T0368704

STORIES FROM BEHIND THE CURTAIN,
ANECDOTES OF A RECUPERATING PASTOR

CHARLES CLINT HITTLE

WESTBOW
PRESS®
A DIVISION OF THOMAS NELSON
& ZONDERVAN

WestBow Press books may be ordered through booksellers or by contacting:

WestBow Press
A Division of Thomas Nelson & Zondervan
1663 Liberty Drive
Bloomington, IN 47403
www.westbowpress.com
844-714-3454

ISBN: 979-8-3850-3636-3 (sc)
ISBN: 979-8-3850-3637-0 (e)

Library of Congress Control Number: 2024921772

Print information available on the last page.

WestBow Press rev. date: 10/21/2024

WELCOME

Welcome reader to the chaotic world of my ADHD brain. My desire in writing down these stories and poems, is to bring you a little laughter, some motivation, some joy, and maybe even a little bit of hope. I truly hope you find humor, encouragement, and faith in these pages. These stories are true and retold to the best of my ability.

Blessings and peace

Charles Clint Hittle

FIRST A WARNING

My thoughts and stories will contain the following:

Spiritual hygiene, Psychological nudity, Scientific inebriation,
Intellectual lunacy and Relational inaccuracies,
but read on anyway.
I can promise to be rationally irrational, logically
illogical, and emotionally emotionless.
So
In the interest of your interest,
I will subject you to this subject.
I hope you do not mind; it is from my mind.
So, in the spirit of The Spirit,
it's about He who oversees those overseas.
Its mostly about Him, He never
overlooked an overlook.
He leaves the leaves,
He brushed the brush.
He shed the sheds,
He bears with the bears.
He steers the steers,
He put the space in space.
He put the spring in spring,
He made the plains plain.
He knows your nose,

and He blocked the blocks.
So
While this is novel,
let us not make it a novel.
Let's Read, Reader!

This Book was edited by Brenda Hittle - Jeff McLeod
Karl Hittle - Karen Rozell – Julee Elkins.

CONTENTS

CONTENTS

CHAPTER ONE

A FUNERAL WITH ELVIS

Some of the most unbelievable days are always those first few months after finishing school and accepting that first position in a ministry. You take that job, and not long after that first day, you realize that knowing a little bit about Greek and Hebrew hasn't equipped you like you thought it would. During my rookie ministry season, fresh out of school and after leaving my construction career, I did a funeral I will never forget, a funeral with Elvis.

The job I had signed up for was with a 501C3 not-for-profit ministry to people with low incomes. I was their first Chaplain/Counselor, and I was as green as they come. I had probably only been in my job for a full three weeks when a woman approached me about doing the funeral of her son. I had met this woman just days prior after we had briefly spoken, and now she seemed so different. She had been trying to get someone to do a "special funeral," but without a church home, she found it hard to find a willing officiant. It was tough for her to get a volunteer for the specific funeral she wanted. She walked up to me and told me about her older son's death and her most recent younger son's death. This desperate mother told me that she needed to have closure for both of these boys, with "one big funeral." Of course, I was flattered and immediately accepted the assignment without asking any questions about the particulars of this gathering. She left out all the details that had alienated the previous funeral officiants and signed me up.

The time finally arrived in a few short days, and I was nervously planning an event for two people I had never met. Along with that difficulty, except for only two brief conversations, there needed to be more communication from the woman. I put on my suit, gathered my wife, and headed out to attend the viewing and conduct the first funeral of my career. As my wife and I walked into the tiny funeral home, it was noticeably apparent I was the only person in a suit. I stood out like an Amish person in an electronics superstore. People stared at me and said, "Well, you must be the preacher." At that point, I noticed that various people were wearing all sorts of interesting costumes, and others were wearing casual clothes, shorts, and flip-flop sandals.

Near the end of this uncomfortable visitation, the father of the boys pulled my wife and me aside to "ask a favor" of me. He told me of the family's long-time connection with a former Las Vegas Elvis impersonator (who had long since retired) and wanted to co-officiate the funeral ceremony with me. The question was, "pastor, would you mind doing this funeral with Elvis?". I must admit I was a bit taken aback, but there was no way to get out now, and I thought to myself, "How bad could it be, right?" I accepted the challenge and listened to the stories of the former glory days of this mystery Elvis entertainer. I then inquired about the identity of "the King" then excused myself to the bathroom so I could search the internet for the man and verify if he was, in fact, "famous." Much to my surprise, he had, in fact, played Vegas many years prior and was one of the premier impersonators there. What struck me as odd was that he had retired many years ago. I remember doing the math as I sat there in my temporary porcelain office and concluded that he was at least seventy years of age.

It wasn't long before I had returned to the tattered gathering space when the door flew open. The room filled with a dusty wind, and there he stood, "Elvis." As he entered the room so did his "entourage". This surreal moment was heightened because they were all calling him "E." To make it even more interesting, he was calling each one by name (not their own name), but the name of a person in the real Elvis' entourage. I wondered if I was hallucinating when he entered the room because he easily weighed four times the rather portly real Elvis and was sporting a skin-tight, white jumpsuit. To say that this white spandex suit was revealing is like saying our planet has a little bit of water on it. My new Elvis, and funeral co-officiant, also had on a big belt almost identical to the one Elvis wore with his similar costume. "E" had jet black hair that Somebody obviously dyed that afternoon and knock-off glasses that looked just like the ones Elvis wore on stage. This faux Elvis had a cape and large mutton chop sideburns just like his idol and even had the same footwear that the King usually wore to perform.

As I stood in shock, watching the entourage work for and attend to faux Elvis serving him food and a beverage, Somebody then told me that I was being summoned to Elvis' side. "E," asked me if I would mind if he sang during the funeral, to which I responded, "Sure, no problem." Then I was informed that he had a bad cold and that he would be lip-syncing to a CD and not actually singing today. "Sure, no problem," again spilled out of my mouth before I caught myself, and then he said what I would hear many times over the course of this day. Now, I know you are anticipating what I am about to say, and you are right. Faux Elvis looked at me and said, "Thank you, thank you very much." I couldn't believe what I had just heard and did my best to contain my shock and laughter as I spun around in retreat to rethink this funeral.

You will have to be patient with me as I try to accurately describe this tiny chapel where we were about to hold the first part of this funeral. I assure you, it makes this part of the story so much better. This place would seat 180 people in two rows of pews, about six people wide and 15 rows deep. The chapel was very traditional but looked like it was set up in a large living room. This room was 30 feet wide and, at best, 45 feet deep. The podium where "Elvis" and

I were supposed to speak was only 5 feet from the first row, which left just enough room to roll a casket into the room at the front. The funny thing about this room is that the loudspeaker for all music and all amplified vocals from the podium was on the opposite side of the front of the room. This speaker configuration made it hard on the row just in front of the podium because they heard the speaker's actual voice before the amplified version echoed out of the speaker at the far right of the room.

This tiny well-paneled, and ornate room was painted white, and all the hard surfaces made even the slightest peep echo throughout this minuscule center for redneck remembrances. Ceiling-hugging crystal-like light fixtures cast their patterns across the popcorn-textured ceiling. Just behind the podium was a metal screen that matched the speaker cover on the other side of the room. Behind the screen on our side was where the funeral director and organist sat hidden. They would instruct and communicate with us through this screen and could no doubt be heard by the front row or two of people. This was why there was no speaker on the left side of the room.

I began the service with a welcome, followed by the opening prayer, and then read the obituary to the crowd, most of whom were seated directly in front of me. I then proceeded to introduce "Elvis." His displeasure was evident when I introduced him using his real name and didn't introduce him as Elvis. Not surprisingly, I'm sure no one was surprised to find out that he was not actually Elvis. As the music began playing, I realized it was an Elvis CD playing, not one of his own albums. Then, much to the amazement of this small group of people, there wasn't the slightest sound coming out of "E." His mouth was moving, but there was no sound. Those seated in the front two rows were staring at "E," unmistakably confused as to why they couldn't actually hear "E." To make things even worse, great sound was being amplified by the loudspeaker on their right. So, the crowd could not only hear the album, but they suddenly realized for

4

themselves that it was the real Elvis' album and that "E" was doing the worst lip-sync job they had ever witnessed.

I don't know if you have ever been in a situation where you were trying to hold back repressed laughter as the pressure increases and the desire to laugh increases exponentially. This was one of those moments. Suddenly, blurts, gaffs, coughs, and quick laughs were bursting out here and there. I mistakenly raised my head just in time to see my wife (who had positioned herself at the back of the room) lying down in the pew, clutching her face.

The space between "E" and me was very small, which only magnified the pressure. I sat on a tiny pew just behind the podium and within a foot or two of the backside of this rotund entertainer. I grappled within myself, "I can't laugh; I must not laugh, or he will hear me; I'm only inches away from the man." I conjured up memories of my grandmother's funeral. I thought of the time I broke my collarbone. I attempted to think of anything except what was going on, but it didn't work. I caught another glimpse of my wife as she was reading the obituary over and over and then fell forward again with her head in her lap clutching her face. Then, I could no longer restrain myself, and there it was, the laugh I thought I could contain. Then our entertainer made the lip sync tragedy even worse by turning to look at me and not continuing to move his lips. Of course, the CD continued the beautiful music of the real Elvis and this sent the audience into a tailspin, with almost no hope for recovery.

I did my best to recover as I stood to do my job. The first song was over and surely now I could regain my composure and lead this motley group along the funeral agenda. This of course is what I thought, but when I saw the faces of those precious people in the first three or four rows, I sputtered and cracked up again. This let the entire lot of them loose from the prison of decorum they had been doing their best to stay in. They surely were thinking "if the Pastor is laughing, then so can I."

To say that the family was upset would be a vast understatement.

The scowl on the father's face was very pronounced as he folded his arms over his chest. I stated the only recovery styled line that popped in my stress filled mind "isn't it great to be able to laugh as we celebrate Timmy and Jimmy's lives. "They would love to know that we didn't just mourn but that we had a good time today". After saying that, it seemed to settle the crowd as people agreed out loud.

Somehow, we got composed enough to transition through the funeral a bit further and when it came to the portion where we would open the microphone up for those who would like to share. I said "please tell us a funny story or favorite saying you experienced from knowing these two young men." I had heard from other pastors that this was a great tactic to use when you knew very little about the deceased. I readied my pen and pad as I assumed, I would hear some words of encouragement, or maybe a human quality that I could brag about later in my portion of the funeral. The first story was about a wild drunken party where one of the boys had passed out, and his brother had taken his clothes off and was walking around naked. Ok, I told myself there was nothing I could comment on there. The second story was so full of profanity I couldn't find any words to write down. I began to panic, because I wasn't getting the material I needed to round out my eulogy. The stories were funny, yet at the same time they didn't seem to be honoring anyone. It hit me like a flash from above that since we were celebrating, I should invite "E" to say a few words since he was a family friend. As I sat there in a small chair next to the small pew that he filled to most of its capacity I whispered I would be honored if you would share a story "E". Oh no, oh wow, I slipped, I called him E, oh well.

Our faux Elvis began with stories of his career, he regaled us with tales of his fame and a quick mention of his introduction to this family. "Good" I said to myself, "it took a while but he is finally going to talk about the young men. Wait, what?" "E" just said, "Thank you, thank you very much," and then plopped down in the small pew, obviously spent from his efforts. I was now lost and reeling, I felt "E" had just dropped out in mid-sentence and left me hanging. My mind was racing as I stood, and I said, "What have we heard here today?" I told the crowd that I had realized these men were good friends to them all to which everyone agreed. I then said "isn't great to be able to celebrate lives lived?" "Now that was deep," I said to myself. Somehow, I stumbled, fumbled and mumbled my way through the next few minutes and made it to the second and last lip-sync performance of our special guest. It wasn't long before this portion of the funeral concluded and we transitioned to what I thought would be a graveside service of sorts.

"This portion of the funeral was absolutely the most surreal portion by far," I said to myself as we walked into the next room for instructions for our next experience. I only thought I had seen bazar. At this juncture the only thing I knew was that the two young men had been cremated. We were all then informed that we would be adjourning and regathering at the local lake to spread the young men's ashes. As the plans were unfolding, I was told that there was a family houseboat that we would be riding the waves in, and that they had a whole ceremony planned to honor "the boys." It only furthered my suspicions that I had gotten myself into something I couldn't escape. I didn't fear for my life immediately, but when I saw the family's "house boat" I truly began to pray that we would return safely.

To call this water vessel a houseboat is only comparable to calling a bag of pork-rinds "Hors d'oeuvres" or ketchup a "fancy sauce". It was like being held captive on a flotation device. I was called aside and told that we were going to stay on this "boat" after the funeral to watch the sunset. I stared at my watch and calculated that it would it be at least four hours before the sun would even begin its descent. I wasn't sure what to do, but I was going to do my best to stay away from "E." They had placed our former Vegas showman in the center of the boat in a chair, and I assumed this was a form of ballast, or a load leveling attempt to keep us all safe. I then browsed through the onboard snacks that would be my supper. Included in our feast were crackers, squirt cheese, pickles, big bags of chips (with nothing to dip them in), and some bread. I made a cheese, chips, and pickle sandwich. I felt as though I had conquered this first obstacle, and then I was summoned to the rear deck of the boat.

There was hardly enough room for almost everyone to crowd into the rear area of this houseboat. Luckily for all of us, "E" stayed in his position as someone made him a sandwich that he had seen me invent. I was petitioned to pray and open up this portion of the ceremony, so I did. It was then that I noticed what appeared to be two handmade wooden crates on each corner of the back of our boat. The crates looked as though they were made from some old fence material and had some small slits between the slats they were made of. After my prayer the mother produced two cremation urns that held the remains of her two boys. As she began to speak, she sat one urn on the right side of the boat and one on the left. She continued to address the crowd rather loudly, and told them that the ceremony would now begin. She said that as a tribute to each boy, before the ashes were cast into the lake, that we were going to release some birds. Now I knew what the two homemade cages were on the corners of the boat. I remember thinking that this was going to finally bring some class to the funeral and to this evening. I saw in my mind a fluttering mass of white doves flying off over the lake as the crates were lifted. I envisioned these symbols of peace gliding effortlessly into the cloudless sky as a beautiful memorial of purity and new life. Then the real release began. As crate number one was lifted all manner of birds screamed and fought to fly in any direction and away from the other birds. It was as if the family had (somehow) trapped sparrows, scissor-tails, and all manner of wild birds. I even saw a crow in the mix. This stirred up the inhabitants of the other box. I don't know if politeness or confusion caused the funeral guests to applaud, but I joined them for some reason.

The father then handed the first urn to the mother as they prepared to spread the first ashes. The lid of the urn took some diligent effort to remove and then the great moment was here. Before I conclude, I need to pause and explain something to those who are not used to seeing and or dealing with cremains. The truth is, no matter what they are delivered to you, the actual ashes are in a very strong plastic bag inside the box or urn; back to the story. So, with the lid removed, the base portion was angled back in such a way as to shovel-throw these first ashes into the lake. What followed was mass hysteria. The bag containing the ashes flew out of the urn and landed with a PLOP a fair distance out in the calm lake water. Suddenly the mom erupted with, "Oh my goodness, someone get Timmy." You have never seen so many people scramble for a stick or a pole to rake Timmy back to and into our boat. After feverish effort, Timmy was retrieved and the mom asked me to pray for the ceremony again, so I did. This time the spreading of the newly dried and opened ashes went well as the nice breeze carried them out into the lake beyond our boat.

Then, the time to spread Jimmy's ashes came, so in a similar fashion, we started with releasing birds. It should be noted there were birds in this box that I had never seen before, and this time, feathers went everywhere. The time came to focus on the other son, so the urn and the bag were opened. I also think that only I seemed to be thinking about the fact that the wind was in our faces on this side of the boat. Just as I had this thought, Mom let the ashes go. I don't know if it was the devil who gave a little extra gust of wind at that moment, or maybe just a redneck form of Murphy's law, but Jimmy came blowing back into all of our faces. Luckily for me my mouth was mostly closed, others were not so lucky. People were coughing and spitting Jimmy into the lake as mom erupted with "oh my goodness Jimmy" and "that's just Jimmy, always the prankster." I remember thinking that there was another explanation for the storm of ashes, which squarely fits into the category of the unintelligent, or even poor planning, but our host seemed to think it was a prank done by her deceased son.

Finally, the awkwardness subsided, and the family broke into storytelling mode with even more raunchy stories than they had shared in our open mike portion of the funeral. Now the tequila was flowing like water and the reasons for "a shot" were getting more and more insane. A cannonball contest was formulated and began from the upper deck of the boat. I wondered if I would ever see land again. I stood on the side of the boat wondering if I could swim that far if the ship went down. Moments later, I had to talk my wife out of attempting that same swim. I could see myself allowing my wife to float on a big chunk of the boats hull as I held her hand (like a scene from the movie Titanic). I stood there in my suit sweating as "E" unzipped his white stretchy suit down to his hairy belly button. I remember thinking that he would win the cannonball competition if I could somehow talk him into it. With my coaching and his girth we were sure to win but he just sat back down and asked for more food.

I then enquired if my wife and I could be dropped at the closest dock so that we might go home. I remember the reply like it was yesterday, "Oh no, pastor, we only have enough gas to go in once." Well, there I was stuck for hours sweating in my suit trying to apologize to my wife for the umpteenth time. I thought I might buy them some gas, but being new at this "non-paying funeral" and on a new salary that was 89% less than my former salary, I just decided to wait it out.

Just when I thought it couldn't possibly get any worse, I was summoned by faux Elvis. He had called me to his center position in the boat for something very important. "E" had me bend down so others wouldn't hear what he would say. I will never forget the confused feelings I had as he told me how he wanted his next sandwich made and what he wanted to drink. I let him finish his order, and then I bent back into position so that, in the same way, others would not hear what I was about to say. Now, hear my heart here: I was new and sweaty, my wife was angry, and I was broke. The next thing that spilled from my lips I am not proud of, and yet somehow it needed to be said. I told faux Elvis (in a slight whisper) to "get up and get it himself." Now look, I was frustrated! I was full up on this mega-long free duty, and I was new at this job (and not doing very good, I know)

Lastly, I knew I needed to redeem myself in the eyes of all concerned, so I decided to go outside and mingle. What happened next got me a hero's status with the family and won me a second-place mention. I decided I was far too sweaty to worry about decorum any longer. I took everything out of my pockets, handed them to my wife, and in full suit I climbed to the top of that rickety "houseboat" and did the cannonball of my life. Needless to say, this was the topic of conversation for the balance of our trip and one act that garnered many comments about how cool I was. I pretty much ruined my suit, but after all I had gone through that day, it was worth it!

We are to rejoice with those who rejoice and to mourn with those who mourn (Rom 12:15), but we are also to become all things to all people so that one might be saved.

(1 Cor 9:22). I have done countless more funerals since then, although none quite as fun or strange. (Well, there might be another one, but that's a different story.) I have learned many lessons in this weird but wonderful life. One lesson that sticks with me is that people are just regular, well-meaning versions of life's lessons and experiences, and we are all just as messed up as the others. So be forgiving and loving and serve others with all your heart, and try not to call them fat asses!

CHAPTER TWO

A DISEASE COMMON TO MAN

I felt tranquil that morning as I stood on the porch and watched the sun begin to peek over the purple hills in the distance. I stood sipping my hot tea and started scanning the yard for the morning paper. I assumed the day would begin as all the others had before. As was my daily routine, I made my way to my favorite chair, searched through the paper, and browsed it as I waited for my family to be jolted awake by their own individual alarm clocks. I will never forget the lump that formed in my throat as I opened the paper and read the headlines. "Disease infects thousands" caught my attention as my eyes darted across the page. I reached for the chair and sat down with a sigh as I read on about the neighboring states and their problems with this disease. It shocked me to realize that such a thing could really invade this country of ours. The article explained that the sickness was contracted by eating fruit, and it was causing crippling results. "Scientists are baffled," I read aloud as I chased each word, trying to determine how and why such a disease could so easily threaten us. That morning was seared into my memory as I sat shocked and wondered if we would have to deal with this disease in our state.

It wasn't long before my fears were realized as one county after another found that they, too, were showing signs of the virus. This plague spread like wildfire. At first, it was contracted by eating fruit, but then it spread in a multitude of ways. My town was buzzing with theories about the disorder's cause and origin. Some said it was the punishment of God, while others said it was an attack from our enemy. All I knew was that I was troubled about what might happen to my family and me.

As the days passed, I read each morning's news as the disease continued to creep ever closer to us. Soon, the reports placed it just miles away. That spurred me to take a closer look at the symptoms and causes. As it closed in on my home, we found ourselves praying, which we had seldom done before. Upon further study, I found that the disease could be caught in several ways and almost anywhere imaginable. I remember thinking that no one would be immune to its wrath. I watched as my neighbors fell one by one from its crippling effects. I saw them limping, blind, and burdened by many other things, just beaten down by this relentless sickness. I saw it overtake my wife, and when I first felt its sting, the remorse was debilitating. As it swept across our town, there were casualties from car wrecks, suicides, and drug overdoses by those who attempted to relieve the pain that it wreaked. Yes, the disease was here, and it was as big as life itself.

Amidst this pummeling onslaught, a few observations stood out in my mind as I made my daily trek to the front porch in search of the ever-evasive newspaper. I tracked the disease all over our fine city. I noticed that some held out longer than others before contracting it and even held it off for quite a while. I noticed that some people were affected in a grandiose way, which really made it hard on their families. Some folks were only slightly infected, chiefly because of their efforts to ward off its various side effects. I found that studying about it helped me and others from catching yet another strain or form of it. Indeed, it had many forms and strains and multiple ways to infiltrate a person over and over. Some were so impacted that their lives were consumed with enduring and preventing the destruction.

I don't remember the exact moment when it dawned on me, but I do remember it was a Sunday when I realized my whole town was now infected. There was only one person who had not been captured by its effects. I read that morning that the next-to-last person had succumbed to the disease. As each of the last and few remaining people in our country contracted it, the papers would report their names. Finally, the virus had settled itself, and the last two remaining people in the whole country had fallen to its encroachment. Only one person remained without its pain and horror, and that person was my son.

As Scientists from around the globe came to our little town to study my son, I could not help but think about what might lie ahead. In the following weeks, I went to the front porch each morning and found myself guessing what the headlines would pronounce. Soon, it became far too real as I opened the paper one morning and read the headline that I had dreaded would be made public: "Texas Boy has no disease."Well, that was one person left, and it was my son, and now the whole world knew it.

The Authorities never came to the house unless they were covered entirely in hazmat-styled suits, hoods, and gloves. These scientists ran test after test, poking, probing, and tormenting my son. They constantly questioned him and required him to perform various tasks. It was as though they hated him for his immunity, yet they demanded answers at the same time. Then, the inevitable day came- the dreaded day I had knowingly and carefully planned for. They made it clear: they wanted his blood. Through all their tests and analysis, they realized the only solution was my son's blood. They called us together as a family to give us the news. "Mr. Chuck," they said, "we need your son's blood to create the serum that will save humankind. The answer is in His blood, and we need all of it!" "What?"

I asked. "Did you say all?". "Yes," they brashly declared- "your son must die for us all to be saved." I shouted, "Get out of my house, just get out of here!" Then an innocent little voice, a still small voice said "it's ok dad I will do it." "What?" I asked. "Yes, I will willingly do it. "After all," he bravely said, "if I do, then the world will be able to live." I couldn't believe what I was hearing. I was so proud and shocked as I accompanied him to the research vehicle to give his blood and his life. As he neared the end, I couldn't watch any longer, so I turned my head as his life slipped away, and he was gone. The coming days were so complicated that I don't have words to express what took place. I watched as many in my town just entirely and almost instantly recovered. I would talk to them and bring up my son's name, and they would stare at me as though they were confused and ask, "Who?". They didn't even know his name! I began to organize rallies to celebrate his gift to the world. I organized a celebration one Sunday to celebrate his gift to our town. To my shock and dismay, only about 29% of the city showed up. To make things worse, some in attendance complained about the music, others slept, and others played games on their cell phones during the celebration. Some people showed up late; others were there only to see if there was any free stuff. I couldn't believe that my son gave his life for theirs, and far too many did not care to celebrate their renewal, healing, cleansing, and freedom. I found some people in the venue's lobby networking and trying to sell their wares. Others stood outside smoking and complaining that the music I had chosen was not their type or too loud. I wanted to shout, "ARE YOU KIDDING ME?" HE GAVE HIS LIFE FOR YOU. COME ON!" I was astonished they couldn't just put themselves aside for a few minutes to honor the life-giving gift that they had received.

Centuries have passed since that great day, and some still remember and celebrate my son's life-giving gift. I am always at those locations to celebrate with those who acknowledge this gift and remember all that it means to millions worldwide. Many books have been written about this priceless gift and many people teach of His generosity and bravery. I trust by now, dear reader, you understand that he gave his life to cure the disease that everyone has. And think-it all started with eating a piece of fruit.

CHAPTER THREE

A SPIDER WHO GOT TO KNOW ME BEFORE HE DIED

I have to start by saying I am deathly afraid of Spiders. In my house, my wife has to do all of the spider killing. Snakes don't really bother me because they can't crawl on me without my knowledge. This phobia comes from my childhood. I have two fears: dentists and spiders, and I'm not sure which scares me the most. That sounds like a leader for another story, ha-ha.

This story begins shortly after I was employed at my third ministry job. I started as the Children's, Singles, and Counseling Pastor, so it's a good thing I can multitask. Shortly after, the Youth Ministry was also added to my plate, and I was to hire people to replace myself slowly so that I could move up to the vacant Associate Pastor position.

The elderly church secretary had called the pest control man the previous Friday to come out to the church and spray. Before I continue, there are four very important points I must make. First, the church property was infested with spiders in all six buildings. Second, our story unfolds very early in the morning. Third, the church secretary was the mother-in-law of the Senior Pastor. Fourth, did I say I am afraid of spiders?

After much begging on Friday, the pest man was called to come out on Monday morning. He must have had a bunch on his plate, so he showed up very early to spray. He called the secretary to tell her someone needed to be there so he could spray the interiors of the buildings as requested. As the secretary told this gentleman I would arrive soon, I pulled up in my truck. The pest man stood by his truck on his phone as I stepped out of mine. I heard him ask, "What does the pastor look like?" My description matched me reasonably well, but probably not exactly because, to be completely forthright, our secretary's eyesight wasn't very good. I heard him say, "I think this is him," as I rounded the corner and quickly stuck my key in the lock to open the main building door.

Before I continue, I need to slow the story down for a moment so that you can visualize the situation in your mind's eye. As I rounded the corner of the building with my eyes fixed on the Exterminator, I quickly glanced down at the lock to insert my key. But then my gaze was back on our pest control guest as I yelled to him, "Let me set my stuff down, and I will open all the buildings for you." What happened next reveals I wasn't quite as sanctified as I thought, and I genuinely have no good excuse for it. What transpired took me back at least two decades to a time when my construction job site behavior was nothing remotely appropriate on our church property. Try to visualize this if you can. Like an enemy setting up base camp, a BIG wolf spider had built its nest in the corner of the front door jamb of the main building. This was the closest corner to me and slightly above the deadbolt I had just unlocked. I'm sure he was finishing his nightly smorgasbord of bugs attracted by the exterior light just to the left of our doorway. So, as I opened the door while looking back at our Pest Guest while having just spoken to him, I immediately turned and walked straight into its well-constructed web.

Mr. Wolf was sitting right in the middle of said web with his back to me, face high, minding his own business. What happened next is like the stuff of almost any horror film ever made, and it was undeniably one of the most terrifying things thus far in my life. As I walked through the seeming impenetrable web, it wrapped around my skull, implanting the now gargantuan Mr. Wolf squarely on my face. His hairy back was on my mouth, nose, and cheek. My first reaction would make any Olympic athlete very proud. I jumped backward so far that I cleared the front walkway and landed in the grass out front. As I flew through the air, I was swatting my face with the enthusiasm that only someone kissing a giant, rather hairy spider could accomplish. My glasses flew one way as I flew backward in the opposite direction. Then, my inexplicable and inexcusable former Construction Worker manifested in full display: I uttered a string of curse words that began with "mother", went through "sons," and ended with feces. I strung those words together in no logical or grammatically correct structure, but as I stood there cursing like a madman, scrubbing and cursing, I heard the pest man tell our aged secretary, "I don't think this is the pastor."

I will never forget the look on his face as I approached him and his truck. He stayed behind the door of his truck (I'm sure to shield himself) so that he could jump into the safety of the vehicle if I got too close. He blurted out with a mix of fear and amazement, "My God, man, what just happened to you?" I had no explanation other than my abject fear of spiders, and he had no sympathy. Then he said, "Good thing it's early; you wouldn't want your Pastor to hear you go on like that!" I will also never forget the look on his face when I explained to him that I was the Pastor. That face could be made into a viral social media meme today!

We should all remember that we are human and that we all have planks in our eyes at times. (Matt 7:3-4) Some lose control over small things; others have gained control through disciplined mental transformation over more significant things. I still have a few fears, but my language has improved somewhat, ha-ha. Let's purpose in our hearts to not judge by outward appearances and evaluate people because they are our neighbors and could be our friends.

I am currently still in counseling because of this event, and maybe someday soon, I will achieve victory, and then my wife will no longer have to do all the spider killing in our home.

CHAPTER FOUR

A DENTED FENDER AND TOTAL SURRENDER

I want to tell you a story. This story concerns one of automobile history's worst and most dangerous periods. There was a time (at least in Dallas, TX) when it wasn't safe to venture out onto the roads without fear of bodily harm. Let me begin by explaining this dangerous time. Similar to many others my age, it was the 24 months that followed my 16th birthday. It's no exaggeration to describe it as twenty-four months of pure danger as I began to drive my mother's only car, which happened to be the family's only car. The truth is stranger than fiction, so the truth is these were the months in my life in which I wrecked that car five and one-half times. "How in the world can you wreck a car halfway," you ask. This illustrious feat can only be accomplished by barely leaving the door open while backing the car out of the garage. This allows the car door to be wedged into that small portion of the wall that sticks out a couple of feet on each side. Those walls were apparently put there to remove a car's door if done with the skill that only accompanies adolescent drivers.

I can almost hear you laughing as I write these words. And at the risk of adding more fuel to fire your laughter (this is nearly unbelievable), I also wrecked Mom's car on the way home from picking it up from the body shop, where it was being repaired from my previous wreck. I was carefully instructed to pick up the car that summer day, and I told one of my friends to drop me off at the body shop on his way to work that morning. My mother had ridden the bus to her downtown job and had left me to find a ride and retrieve the car. And to be completely transparent, I'm sure that my early morning departure to retrieve the car saw me hung over from something I had partook in the previous evening. In those days (well before God and my lovely wife), more often than not, most evenings, I imbibed or inhaled an illegal substance to self-medicate to ease the pains of my childhood.

I remember walking to a payphone (yes, this was before cell phones) to call my Mom after I had nodded off and run right through a stop sign. This small faux pas placed me on a collision course with Mrs. Average Citizen, who thought she could safely cross the intersection. As I called my Mom, I felt safer than usual since she was miles away. I remember thinking she was about to reach through the phone and kill me barehanded. At one point, I could almost feel her hands around my neck as I listened to her entirely plausible threats.

What made this unusual is that amid all this mayhem after each collision, Mom would stand by the door to her newly fixed car just before we would embark on a journey together. She would look at me squarely and ask, "Do you want me to drive, or do you want to?" I thought this option would stop after a couple of wrecks, but it did not. The first time this happened, I thought it was a trick to get me to come around to the driver's side of the car to retrieve the keys. I knew for sure that as I got close enough, she would beat me senseless while asking, "Surely you don't think you are going to ever drive my car again, do you?" Yet, each time, I was tossed the keys and stood there dumbfounded and confused. Every single time, I would jump behind the wheel, and off we would go, with me not understanding the great things being taught to me.

Then, one day, many years later, I felt that the Lord just dropped a thought in my brain. I was driving my new car along a road when

He said, "Life is a lot like your car story." "How so, Lord," I asked aloud, unaware I would soon pull over to cry and reflect. Once I regained my composure, these thoughts poured into my mind: We "drive" through this life doing our jobs, down our roads while wrecking our lives occasionally. Some people get totaled; others only partially, but a wreck is a wreck. Then God said, "You know I say that to you every morning." "What is that, Lord?" I ask. He said, "Chuck, do you want me to drive, or do you want to?" I realized that most mornings, I would say, "No thanks, Lord; I can handle it; you remember, I am a good driver, a really good driver." Of course, with the same love my mother showed me, God would say, "OK."

Nowadays, when my feet hit the floor in the morning, I'll say out loud, "You drive, Lord; I'm with you. I'll study the map (Bible)." I intentionally surrender to His plan and directions, His promptings and destination for the day, and off we go. I don't try to navigate or copilot; I ride along and enjoy my friend.

That old yellow Ford Galaxy 500 four-door was one tough car. I only wish I were that tough. These days, I counsel people in my spiritual body shop when their lives are wrecked or they have the occasional fender bender. I often think back on those first 24 months of mayhem, and I am happy to be here to straighten out a fender or help with surrender.

CHAPTER FIVE

FISHING FOR ANSWERS

I am sitting in this old yellow chair, rocking and thinking back on those yesterdays that have come and gone. The lights in my living room are purposefully dimmed so, not to awaken anyone else in the house. My only companion right now is a four-year-old boy who only exists in my mind. Even though the dark paneling mostly absorbs the reading lamp's golden glowing light, I can see him with the most incredible detail. Yes, if I close my eyes and lean my head back, I can pull it all into my mind's eye. I can even smell those outdoor smells: the damp leaves, the moist ground, and even that specific smell a tackle box seems to get after a couple of good years of service.

I remember so well my reaction that afternoon was to ask God if I had ever asked questions with overly obvious answers. I remember thinking that we must learn, and as we grow in the Lord, we must also ask some funny questions. I remember asking God many times why my dad had to leave us, yet I never got any answers. I also recollect as I looked at my four-year-old in his cute little shoes and rolled-up jeans (purposefully rolled because he was a little wider than he was tall) and asked questions. Questions like those still bother me: How could a man leave his family, and why couldn't I when far too many others do?

I couldn't understand then, and I can't now understand why my dad left us. I sit here in my thinking chair, my throne in my own home. Even now, that four-year-old that I couldn't leave is asleep in his room; he has just put on about thirty years and a hundred forty pounds and is sleeping in his own home. That four-year-old, who is unrecognizable to most, is still there. I see him sometimes in a quick glance or a happy moment, and always when he is sick or needs some love or advice.

"Here we are, bub," I said to him. Yes, I can still see his sweet little face, especially if I lean my head back and close my eyes. As I unbuckle his seatbelt and walk around to open his car door, I can hear myself say, "Hey, let's go fishing, my friend, let's go catch a big-un, big-un; come on. You carry these two fishing rods, and Daddy will carry all this other stuff." As I gave him all that he could manage, it must've been hard to carry more than two things while wearing the oversized sunglasses and new fishing hat I had just given him. It was even more comical because the hat and glasses were too big for him, and they'd slip and slide all over his head with each step. "Can you get those Bud?" I asked as I grabbed the chairs, the tackle boxes, the drink cooler, two more fishing rods, and my hat and glasses. It should go without saying that it was a must we both had the same equipment as each other, or we just wouldn't be able to catch fish. At least that is how it was presented to me so that I would buy the new hat and glasses. So off we go, finally on our way; slowly, I lead, being careful not to run off and leave my best buddy behind. Out in front, I trudged along, knocking down spider webs, forging the trail, and fishing on my mind, memories in the making.

"What was that?" I said as I heard a noise. Was it me? I was almost asleep. "I wonder if the light is too bright or if I am waking up the whole house with my late-night session? Maybe I should return to bed and recall this memory some other time. No, I think I will go just a minute or two longer, and then I will go by his picture in the hall on my way back to bed. As for now, I will lean my head back and close my eyes for one more moment of memories."

"Watch out for that hole, don't step in it!" I shouted back as I forged along. I remember my steady gate, guiding instructions, and fear when I heard two fishing poles crash to the ground. I must have spun around with that atomic fear that dads get when the protector snaps into place. As I quickly turned back to survey the situation, I asked him, "Bud, are you, all right?" I then realized I was almost alone on the path. My four-year-old, with the fishing rods at his feet, stood way back down the trail. "Get those rods, buddy, and come on," I shouted in his direction, but I received no reply. I saw him there with his hands on his hips, his eyes cast upward, turning one way then another, and a curious look on his little hat-covered head. "Come on, buddy, let's go," I said to him, assuming it would break his trance and that he would resume the mission with me. Nothing, no movement, so again I spoke to him. "Come on, bud," I said, only this time I got a reply, "Dad, come here," he said and continued his puzzled stance. "Dad, come here," he said," it's important. " He added that emphasis to get me to travel the distance back to him without aggravation. So, off I went back down the damp trail to carry the other two rods, or better yet, to carry him as well. I began to check him for damage and then knelt on one knee by this miniature version of me. It was then I heard one of the greatest questions I have ever heard. It was one of those invaluable questions that not even a professional writer but only a child could dream up. " Daddy," he asked as he looked skyward, "is this the woods or just a bunch of trees?" He stood there very seriously with a furrowed brow and his hands in the thinking position on his hips. Trying not to laugh, I replied, "I think it's the woods, my friend." As I gathered our stuff, rods and all, I encouraged him, "Come on, buddy, let's go fishing."

In that seemingly insignificant moment, I learned something-something about God and me. God loves all my questions and all our times together, just like I love the times with my Son. And in the same way, He only gives me what I can carry and manage as I grow. I have learned He is ready (even more so than me) to come and get me restarted and back on the path. He refocuses me towards the goal ahead and will carry me if need be while I rest. I also realized that, unlike my earthly Father, He would never leave me or forsake me.

I can't express how powerful and comforting this truth is that I learned from one little question from my precious four-year-old Son that day. That simple question taught me so much about God and me and the father-son relationship we have with each other. I didn't do much fishing that day because I mostly sat and thought. I sometimes found myself with my head back, and my eyes closed. I thanked God for my Son and my relationship with him and recounted the day and the lessons learned.

"Well, come on, son," I heard as I sat up in my old yellow chair. "Goodnight, Dad," I said to the Lord as I stood and turned off that old reading light and stumbled towards the back of the house. Making my way back to our bedroom, I took another look at that picture of my little fishing buddy. I don't think I woke anyone up with my light, my memories, or my noise. And now, I am looking forward to the same kind of peaceful slumber that my Son feels and enjoys. It's the kind of peaceful sleep we can only get when we're safe under our Father's protection, secure in His arms, tucked in, and warm. "Lord, come here; it's important," I said as I chuckled a little, leaned my head back, and closed my eyes.

CHAPTER SIX

THE BOX

As a young man, I found that I had a tremendous amount of unforgivness in my heart at an early age. This contempt was partially there because, at an early age, my dad had just up and left me and my brother. I was eight, my brother was two, and I remember thinking that we had it pretty bad because of his departure. My mother, brother, and I left our town and moved to Dallas to live with my grandmother. I was one of two kids that had a divorced parent, and in those days, it made you a bit of an outcast.

I will never forget the feeling of abandonment when my dad showed up at my house with his "new son." Feelings of hatred consumed my tiny mind as he fumbled through the introduction of my new half-brother. I had no hatred for my brother, just for the "father" standing there trying to make the introduction seem OK. I remember thinking that all this was my fault, that my Father hated me, and that he had to go elsewhere and start a new family with a son he loved. I know that this part of the story is challenging and, trust me, painful for yours truly, but it is essential to understand that I was in quite a predicament before I met my real Father.

I can still feel the pain as my various friends' well-meaning fathers offered me advice and reminded me that I didn't have a dad. I remember that everyone's dad participated in Boy Scouts, and I was alone. As the years went by, I lacked so much that I did horrible things for attention; trying to reach hero status with my friends was the all-important goal. I can tell you that hatred began to build as I dreamed of growing up enough and growing tough enough to enact my imagined revenge on my Father.

Then I heard about a young boy named Tim. Tim's mom and dad were killed in some tragic car accident, so little Tim was sent to live with a blood relative who had accepted his custody. This relative had some mental disorder and actually disliked children. Consequently, little Tim, from his early age up to about eight, had been mad to live in a four-foot square box in the living room of this relative. Tim had to get used to this "out of sight, out of mind" model, and there were no options.

Little Tim was only allowed to come out of the box twice a week and then only to see the inside of the house. There was no interaction with friends, no toys, just one TV show while he cleaned his structure and then back in the box. Timmy was fed through a slot mid-way up in the door of his lock box and was told to remain quiet at all times. Tim's bathroom was a tray full of cat litter slid on the floor through a lower slot in that same door. Nobody for years knew he was there, no friends, no family, no neighbors, just his relative and their orders to be silent.

After hearing the story, I found myself thinking I was doing pretty good. I felt as though I didn't have it so bad. I remember wondering how someone could do that to the one they love. I would refer to the story in my mind over and over when things were tough and say to myself, "Well, at least I don't have it as bad as Tim." I was comforted by these thoughts, but at the same time, I felt bad about feeling a bit of relief from someone else tragedy.

Tim was a captive, silently watching as things took place. He was only shown love occasionally and was constantly subjected to whatever was happening while silently observing from his relegated spot.

Years later, as I drove home from my construction job, I was talking to my real Father. This story popped into my mind as

I prayed to, thanked, worshiped, and questioned Him. I was a young believer at the time, and I was trying to raise two boys in a semi-Godly home without much understanding of the Bible. I recalled the story and felt slightly proud of how well I fathered my boys. I spoke aloud and said, "Well, God, at least I didn't raise them in a box; I must be doing OK." It was then the Lord dropped a thought into my novice brain that caused me to pull my truck over to the side of the road. What He said to me, I'll never forget. He said, "Great son, but you do that to me." "You have me boxed up in your heart, and you take me places I would rather not go." "You tell me to be quiet as you hide me there, but you continue to ask me to feed you through the slot in my box." "You only let me out twice a week, and then it's only to see the inside of the church." "No interaction with your friends, no other place, am I acknowledged. Just get back in the box and be quiet until I need you."

I was unable to drive, speak, or do anything but cry. I found myself living a "churchianity" life and nothing more. My family was lacking because of the box I had created in my heart. I had Jesus boxed away like a Secret Service Christian.

I went home that evening and changed everything. This decision eventually led me to return to school two more times and become a pastor and counselor. My kids and friends know who I live for, and I have totally gotten rid of the box.

I must ask you, have you locked Christ up in your heart? Does anyone Know He is there? Is He your silent captive? If He is, let today be the day God hands you the crowbar. Let Christ reign in His rightful place in your life, above and in all aspects of your life. Un-box him for good, for your family, and for you.

OK, back to Tim, his captivity was eventually discovered through neighbors, prying and looking in windows. Tim was taken from his captor and helped to recover and return to normal life. When he was found, Tim was almost like an animal; he could not speak, but only a few words, and he was not capable of having a normal childhood. Later, after Tim's recovery, he recounted to the physicians and counselors who were helping him that he thought all kids lived in a box. As far as I know, Tim now lives a normal life.

CHAPTER SEVEN

ANGELS UNAWARE /
DROWNING IN BLESSINGS

The story I'm about to convey is almost unbelievable. It's hard for me to believe and I was right there. This story is so amazing that I cry every time I tell it. There are times when I am so blessed it's unimagionable, then other times it seems to go the opposite way. Please hear my heart as you read along and be encouraged as you read this amazing tale.

My wife and I had decided to take a break and go relax. My brother had just moved to the New Braunfels TX area, so we went there to camp and see the sights. We were extra ready to go there because we had been in a very rain-filled month. The rain had finally ended, and the skies were blue. We planned to get a spot near town, but to be in a state park away from the lights and noise. We had been working nonstop for months, and so needed a break. We were almost giddy as we set up the camper and headed out to find an adventure. We decided that we should rent a couple of tubes and float the day away. The funny thing was that most of the float places were closed, the water levels were too high due to the recent rain. Finally, we found a tube rental open, so we stopped.

The owner was sitting there board, no-one was renting because everyone thought all the rentals were closed. We rented our tubes and life jackets and headed to the car for our cooler, sunblock, and sunglasses. I remember almost running to the river, ready to float and unwind in the cool spring water. We sprayed our sunblock on, tied our cooler to one of our tubes, put on our sunglasses and off we went. As we floated, we were trying to remember the instructions of the tube rental man. He had told us of the three waterfalls and how to stay out of danger when we went over the falls. We were so excited that we could not remember which side was the best left or right. It was about this time when I screamed, "Babe, we forgot our lifejackets." At this point, we were way too far down now to go back, so the idea was to play it as safe as possible at each of the falls and to make it safe and easy. The problem was we couldn't remember which side of each of the falls was the safe side.

We were on the river alone, and the power of that water was beyond belief. Neither of us is a good swimmer, and here we are without life jackets. As we approached the first falls, I remember the panic of "which side" and the hope that our choice to go right was, in fact, right.

My tube and I, with cooler in tow, went over first. The turmoil was so intense I knew we had chosen the wrong side. The falls slammed me against the rocks and crashed my head into a hard, smooth rock. Milliseconds after that, the cooler crashed down on me, doing further damage. The interesting thing was I was kicked further to the right into an eddy of sorts. As I stood rubbing my head and clinging to my tube in the chest-deep water, I turned to see the most horrifying sight of my life. My wife had also plummeted over this raging area, and I saw nothing but her tube boiling and flipping at the base of this mighty fall. I yelled her name, and then I saw it, her one arm reaching for her tube, which was just out of her reach. My thought was, as I pushed against the powerful flow, that there was no way for me to get there in time to move her tube over to her flailing arm. I screamed out, "PLEASE, LORD JESUS, I DON'T WANT TO WATCH MY WIFE DROWN TODAY." I couldn't believe this was happening; I pushed so hard, pressing against the power of the water and yelling out to God to save my wife. My heart sank as I made little headway. I was consumed with thoughts of what lay ahead, as they would drag her lifeless body out of the river. PLEASE GOD, I DON'T WANT THIS, PLEASE HELP HER, I yelled with my head down, not wanting to watch what was in front of me.

As I lifted my head this time to for a quick glance between screams, something was different; a young man was standing in the falls, and he was close to my wife. He was a tall, healthy-looking, tanned young man who was standing there looking at me. The water seemed to split around him as he stood there powerfully. I then noticed a near carbon copy of him on the other side of the falls, standing there as well. At this point, I didn't ask questions or even wonder where he came from; I just saw a moment that might save my wife from certain doom.

I said to the young man, "Hey, can you push my wife's tube to her?" "Yes sir," he said as he did exactly that. My wife's flailing arm then found the tube and wrapped itself over the top. The problem then was that the undertow and currents were far too strong for her to pull herself loose from its grasp and to make it to the surface. I could tell it wasn't working, so I said to the young man (who was standing there looking at me), "Hey, can you pull on the tube and pull her loose from the waterfall's undertow?" "Yes, sir?" he said as he did exactly as I asked.

What followed was one of the happiest moments in my life. I continued forward towards my wife as she popped loose from the fall's powerful grasp and got above water. She spit up water and grabbed her first breath, coughing and choking but above the surface of this torrent. We were shaken, to say the least, but we were both so happy to be above water and out of the imminent danger that we had just experienced. I don't think that I will ever again feel that immense amount of relief and joy as I saw her face and watched her breathe air as I continued to push towards her.

These two young men began to see how to meet our every need.

They helped us to the side and walked us to the far, calmer water. They then helped us get re-seated in our tubes and safely on our way downriver. The funny thing was they were now swimming with us in this extremely powerful water and swimming circles around us as we all floated rapidly toward the next set of falls. I wondered how someone could swim against this current so easily, so I asked that question on my lips. Are you guys on the swim team at your school? "No sir," they replied. Then I asked, are you guys out here often? "no sir," they replied again. I wrestled with one thought after another, wondering about these amazing guys. Do you live around here? I said, and again, I was met with just two words: "No sir."

As we approached the next set of falls, we were guided by these two excellent swimmers to come to the left side and walk around the second set of falls. They were taking such good care of my wife, making sure she was safely in her tube. As they swam around us, they spoke for the first time without us initiating a response. One young man said, "Sir, there is one more waterfall ahead, and after that, you both will be fine." I was so appreciative and so overwhelmed with emotion that I wasn't even thinking clearly. All I could do was ask simple questions that were met with "no sir" or "yes sir" as we floated.

After we followed their instructions and were past the third set of falls, one young man spoke again; he said, "Sir, right up here, we will be leaving you and going home." He then told me about the sign that hung over the river that would direct me to the left side and our exit point. About halfway to that sign, they directed us to the left side of the river, where we were to say goodbye. We were overwhelmed with emotions and hugged them both before they left us. These two young men walked over the hill of the river bank and out of our lives.

Just after they had cleared the hilltop, I thought of getting their address and phone number so I could tell their parents what amazing young men they had raised. I told my wife to prepare for the last leg of our journey and that I would be right back. As I cleared the top of the hill, I assumed that I would be met with a parking lot and our two young helpers. I will tell you that what I saw still amazes me to this day. I Saw nothing. There was nothing but a field and a distant tree line. At first, I was confused; where could they have gone? Then it dawned on me.

I stood there momentarily and then returned to my wife at the river. She asked me, "Did you get their names?" I just stood there and said, "No, Ma'am." My wife said, "Their address?" Again, I just replied, "No, Ma'am." Stunned, I said, "Babe, they were gone." "What do you mean they were gone?" she said. We both returned to the top of the hill together to marvel at the distance and the disappearance. As we stood there, she said, "I know their names." "Their names were ere Angel one and Angel two."

We hugged; there were a few tears, and we could barely believe what had happened. For the next few hours, we repeated the story over and over, absolutely amazed at how each moment went. We were more alive than ever before and felt incredibly blessed.

Later that evening, my wife had been saying to herself several times, "Wow, this is the weekend I almost drowned." She said that a still, small voice deep inside her said, "You can frame this weekend however you want." She said that The Lord told her, "You can say that this is the weekend I almost drowned, or this is the weekend that The Lord saved my life." He told her, "You can put this in either frame; tell folks about it either way you choose." After receiving this revelation, she shared it with me, and of course, we chose to give The Lord all the credit.

Later, I was given a message of my own, which came from two scriptures I must share with you. First is

Psalm 91:11-12. NKJV

11 For He shall give His angels charge over you, to keep you in all your ways.

12 In their hands they shall bear you up, lest you dash your foot against a stone.

The second scripture I will share is

Hebrews 1:14 NIV

14 Are not all angels ministering spirits sent to serve those who will inherit salvation?

This was not the first or last time that The Lord would save our lives. As you read through this book you will see another story with similar results. Please know that we are not special and that you are no different. If you are a Child of God then He is watching over you. He has charged his angels to keep you and serve you. Be at peace today, oh and how will you frame the day today?

New International Version. (2011). BibleGateway.com. http://www. biblegateway.com/versions/

New King James Version. BibleGateway.com. http://www.biblegateway. com/versions/

CHAPTER EIGHT

FROM TRASH TO TREASURE / THE OTHER MIRACULOUS STORY

We moved to the northern portion of Texas, near the Oklahoma border, about a year and a half ago. We love returning to the town we lived in for 21 years to visit our favorite stores and restaurants. However, driving the highways and fighting the traffic became tiring, so we found a back route through the countryside. Curvy country roads and incredible scenery surrounded us; we felt this was the best way to travel to and from our old home.

Something miraculous happened on this trip I am writing about. Our lives were saved on our way, and the Lord protected us. Now, I know you've heard this kind of story from me before, but I want you to know that this has happened many times in my life. Obviously, one of those other times is recorded here in this book, in the previous chapter. This time was no different and was a stunning display of the simplicity of God's protection over his children.

This particular day was a beautiful fall day. We were not in any hurry to get to our destination; we just wanted to run some errands and get my wife to her last follow-up appointment with her doctor.

We had just passed through the little town of Forestberg on FM 455, enjoying the temperature and the sunshine. Along the way, there is a double curve in the road, an S-curve, if you will. As we entered this S-curve, we were blind to what was taking place at the other end of the curves.

A dump truck pulling a trash trailer had come along FM 455 at far too great of a speed to handle these curves. This was a small dump truck pulling a rather large trash trailer. The truck and trailer were stacked high with trash, and neither of these mounds were covered. We were about to enter the bottom of this S shape as he entered the top of that same S-shaped double curve. The weight of his overloaded trash trailer was too great to make his first curve at his high rate of speed. As he made this sudden first turn to his left, the trash trailer skidded out to the right of his truck into the grassy roadside. This is approximately when we entered the bottom of the S-curve. The truck driver then had to make the right turn in this area, and the trash trailer reacted like a water skier to a turning boat. Along we came, entering into our first curve, when suddenly in our path was a sliding huge trailer of trash that was now beginning to turn over on top of us.

If I may stop the story right here, I would like to interject a couple of thoughts. Anytime there is something in the roadway ahead of you, your first instinct as you tightly grip the steering wheel is to slam on the brakes. Secondly, (and in this case), time slows down to the point at which everything seems to be in slow motion. Our brains can process information faster than we can imagine, so, at times, this indeed can occur. This slow-motion phenomenon happened to me when I was young. I was riding my 10-speed and talking to the most beautiful girl in our neighborhood. As she drove her car along the road near my home and as I revealed her beauty, I remember very well how time went into slow motion as I hit the park station wagon in the street. I remember how I tumbled over the hood, across the windshield, and up on top of the car in this slow motion I am speaking of. Sorry, it's the ADHD rabbit trail; now, back to our story.

The next portion of the story happened in milliseconds, so slowly that I don't know how to describe it. As I began to lift my foot to slam it down on the brake pedal, I heard a silent voice so loud inside me say, "Drive through there." At this point, the trailer was turning over on top of us, and the trash was spilling out in a large wave of junk that was hard to comprehend. It was a scene unlike those you have seen on TV where surfers are traveling through a giant blue wave like a massive pipeline. This wave of trash was spilling over the top of everything and caused a tunnel-like opening ahead and to the right of us. As these milliseconds ticked by, I knew what my heavenly instructor meant for me to "drive through." Was that very opening.

As my wife screamed in fear, I stomped on the accelerator pedal and shot us through the only opening available. At this point, we were now careening through the grassy roadside at a high rate of speed. Then, the rear end of our car came around and put us into a sideways slide. As the milliseconds continued to unfold, I saw the oncoming traffic sign pole as we headed "broadside" towards it.

If I may again stop the story, I would like to interject something that might be pertinent to this portion of my story. I grew up driving the fast cars of the '70s, driving go-karts, and, of course, the ever-fun slick track go-karts. If you will, I was prepared to react to a slide and how to counter-steer a sideways car because of the power or the slickness of a track. OK, back to the story.

As the pole approached, I snapped the wheel to the other side and brought the rear end around just as we were about to strike the pole. I then realized we were heading towards the lump of a driveway, and I needed to bring the car back around to slide the other way again. Now, though, it was time to go back up onto the street. The slipperiness of the grass and, of course, the traction of the street are two different types of surface. Now, we were in a different kind of spin with squealing tires and some smoke. Providentially, no other cars were coming down the road that day, and we spun to a stop.

If I may stop the story again, I would like to interject something that I feel is pertinent to this portion of the story. Please hear me; I am not saying that I am some kind of professional driver. I will tell you that the instructions and the understanding for this last portion of the story poured into my skull as from above. I am a good driver, but I can't help but ponder on my previous experiences and how they prepared me for this very day. I am overwhelmed with the thoughts of it all, knowing an all-knowing God who prepares his children and most likely uses all things for our good. OK, back to the story.

As we finally sat still in the street, the only thing I could say to my wife was, "Babe, all I heard was drive-through there," and "Do you realize how close we just came to being killed?" As we talked it through for a moment, we began to be worried about the dump truck's driver and whether or not he made it through the horrible swerve of the curves. We both decided to go back and see how he was doing.

As we got back to the bottom of the S-curve, we saw his truck in the distance coming towards us, and his truck looked fine. We knew now that the driver was also fine, and we were all OK. Almost simultaneously, my wife and I saw the trailer, or what appeared to be the trailer. The crashed remains of this vast trailer were strewn all over the area. The trailer was completely destroyed, and it looked like it had been crushed. The weight of the heavier trash in the bottom of the trailer had smashed it against an embankment. The trailer's back doors were gone, and the wheels were disconnected. We both immediately realized that had the brakes been applied in our car, we would be underneath this mound of crushed metal and trash.

The site of this was overwhelming for us both. We sat there speechless and tearful, realizing we had been saved from this massive wreck. The severity of what we saw there was beyond belief.

If you want to hear the entire story and see some visuals, you can see that on my YouTube channel.

Pastor Chuck Hittle sermons and studies

CHAPTER NINE

A DISEASE COMMON TO MAN.

I felt tranquil that morning as I stood on the porch and watched the sun begin to peek over the purple hills in the distance. I stood sipping my hot tea and started scanning the yard for the morning paper. I assumed the day would begin as all the others had before. As was my daily routine, I made my way to my favorite chair, searched through the paper, and browsed it as I waited for my family to be jolted awake by their own individual alarm clocks. I will never forget the lump that formed in my throat as I opened the paper and read the headlines. "Disease infects thousands" caught my attention as my eyes darted across the page. I reached for the chair and sat down with a sigh as I read on about the neighboring states and their problems with this disease. It shocked me to realize that such a thing could really invade this country of ours. The article explained that the sickness was contracted by eating fruit, and it was causing crippling results. "Scientists are baffled," I read aloud as I chased each word, trying to determine how and why such a disease could so easily threaten us. That morning was seared into my memory as I sat shocked and wondered if we would have to deal with this disease in our state.

It wasn't long before my fears were realized as one county after another found that they, too, were showing signs of the virus. This plague spread like wildfire. At first, it was contracted by eating fruit, but then it spread in a multitude of ways. My town was buzzing with theories about the disorder's cause and origin. Some said it was the punishment of God, while others said it was an attack from our enemy. All I knew was that I was troubled about what might happen to my family and me.

As the days passed, I read each morning's news as the disease continued to creep ever closer to us. Soon, the reports placed it just , miles away. That spurred me to take a closer look at the symptoms and causes. As it closed in on my home, we found ourselves praying, which we had seldom done before. Upon further study, I found that the disease could be caught in several ways and almost anywhere imaginable. I remember thinking that no one would be immune to its wrath. I watched as my neighbors fell one by one from its crippling effects. I saw them limping, blind, and burdened by many other things, just beaten down by this relentless sickness. I saw it overtake my wife, and when I first felt its sting, the remorse was debilitating. As it swept across our town, there were casualties from car wrecks, suicides, and drug overdoses by those who attempted to relieve the pain that it wreaked. Yes, the disease was here, and it was as big as life itself.

Amidst this pummeling onslaught, a few observations stood out in my mind as I made my daily trek to the front porch in search of the ever-evasive newspaper. I tracked the disease all over our fine city. I noticed that some held out longer than others before contracting it and even held it off for quite a while. I noticed that some people were affected in a grandiose way, which really made it hard on their families. Some folks were only slightly infected, chiefly because of their efforts to ward off its various side effects. I found that studying about it helped me and others from catching yet another strain or form of it. Indeed, it had many forms and strains and multiple ways to infiltrate a person over and over. Some were so impacted that their lives were consumed with enduring and preventing the destruction.

I don't remember the exact moment when it dawned on me, but I do remember it was a Sunday when I realized my whole town was now infected. There was only one person who had not been captured by its effects. I read that morning that the next-to-last person had succumbed to the disease. As each of the last and few remaining people in our country contracted it, the papers would report their names. Finally, the virus had settled itself, and the last two remaining people in the whole country had fallen to its encroachment. Only one person remained without its pain and horror, and that person was my son.

As Scientists from around the globe came to our little town to study my son, I could not help but think about what might lie ahead. In the following weeks, I went to the front porch each morning and found myself guessing what the headlines would pronounce. Soon, it became far too real as I opened the paper one morning and read the headline that I had dreaded would be made public: "Texas Boy has no disease." Well, that was one person left, and it was my son, and now the whole world knew it.

The Authorities never came to the house unless they were covered entirely in hazmat-styled suits, hoods, and gloves. These scientists ran test after test, poking, probing, and tormenting my son. They constantly questioned him and required him to perform various tasks. It was as though they hated him for his immunity, yet they demanded answers at the same time. Then, the inevitable day came- the dreaded day I had knowingly and carefully planned for. They made it clear: they wanted his blood. Through all their tests and analysis, they realized the only solution was my son's blood. They called us together as a family to give us the news. "Mr. Chuck," they said, "we need your son's blood to create the serum that will save humankind. The answer is in His blood, and we need all of it!" "What?"

I asked. "Did you say all?". "Yes," they brashly declared- "your son must die for us all to be saved." I shouted, "Get out of my house, just get out of here!" Then an innocent little voice, a still small voice said "it's ok dad I will do it." "What?" I asked. "Yes, I will willingly do it. "After all," he bravely said, "if I do, then the world will be able to live." I couldn't believe what I was hearing. I was so proud and shocked as I accompanied him to the research vehicle to give his blood and his life. As he neared the end, I couldn't watch any longer, so I turned my head as his life slipped away, and he was gone.

The coming days were so complicated that I don't have words to express what took place. I watched as many in my town just entirely and almost instantly recovered. I would talk to them and bring up my son's name, and they would stare at me as though they were confused and ask, "Who?". They didn't even know his name! I began to organize rallies to celebrate his gift to the world. I organized a celebration one Sunday to celebrate his gift to our town. To my shock and dismay, only about 29% of the city showed up. To make things worse, some in attendance complained about the music, others slept, and others played games on their cell phones during the celebration. Some people showed up late; others were there only to see if there was any free stuff. I couldn't believe that my son gave his life for theirs, and far too many did not care to celebrate their renewal, healing, cleansing, and freedom. I found some people in the venue's lobby networking and trying to sell their wares. Others stood outside smoking and complaining that the music I had chosen was not their type or too loud. I wanted to shout, **"ARE YOU KIDDING ME?" HE GAVE HIS LIFE FOR YOU. COME ON!"** I was astonished they couldn't just put themselves aside for a few minutes to honor the life-giving gift that they had received.

Centuries have passed since that great day, and some still remember and celebrate my son's life-giving gift. I am always at those locations to celebrate with those who acknowledge this gift and remember all that it means to millions worldwide. Many books have been written about this priceless gift and many people teach of His generosity and bravery. I trust by now, dear reader, you understand that he gave his life to cure the disease that everyone has. And think-it all started with eating a piece of fruit.

POEM 1 CHEEZ ITS

I thought that I would write some words
About something God must have created
I don't know, but maybe you have heard
Cheese and bread are somehow related

This amazing crunchy combination
This snack that always just fits
This cheesy good n salty sensation
The heavenly cracker called Cheez its

The legendary secret mixture
That makes the snack so grand
Has made it a national fixture
One to always have on hand

Get your willpower feeling steady
Put a dietician on retainer
Don't open the box if you're not ready
Cause you're gonna eat the entire container

I bet you can't eat just one
And I am talking box
The consumption is entirely fun
But I hope your cabinets have locks

This addiction brings some weight gain
For your one box a day cracker habit
And then comes the workout pain
Or you'll let your waistline have it

For years I've fought this delicious war
It is a constant fight
You see them when you're in the store
And say 'Oh, for just one bite"

Oh cheez-its you do not play fair
No cracker does taste better
My portion I'll not likely share
Cause I need my dose of cheddar

POEM 2 COFFEE

Early in the morning
when I'm suddenly awakened
I find myself in turmoil
my world has just been shaken.

I'm zombified, and just alive, as I stumble to my station.
With bleary eyes I seek my prize, a cup of motivation.

It's sad to start the day this way, I say to myself so early'
With sleep filled eyes, I realize, the world is all so blurry'

Even though its jumbled
There's the power of this cup
Without it, I would stay inside, and never would get up.

The boiling water loses, all that is my liquid steam
It's not that it is purely love
it may also be caffeine

But as it warms and motivates
I sooner feel I'm steady
I'm starting to initiate
I'm starting to feel ready

And after there is a cup or two, and a little time is spent
I'm ready now to face the world, with liquid encouragement.

Go ahead and drink your cup, you know I'm right, just do it
It is our get up, our go and our fight,
Our Motivationnel fluide.

Charles C Hittle

POEM 3 TWISTY TIE

I think I'll say it
I'd rather die
Then tie-up my bread
With that twisty tie

And that plastic thing
At first, I relented
It's the most horrible thing
That's ever been invented

I like a twirl and a twist
With a good tuck under
Like a real man
If ere you wonder

I refuse the two
Available types
They cause division
They even cause fights

How about you
Do you have an idea?
When she's not around
And she can't see ya

Are you a twist and tuck?
Or do you conform?
Do you have an idea?
That might become the norm

THOUGHT 1. THE MAP

A map is a great thing, but it is not the same as being there. A map of the Bahamas is engaging, fun, and educational, but it isn't nearly as good as the real thing.

A map will tell you where the mountains are, show you the roads to unique places, and warn you of the wilderness areas, but it is no replacement for the real thing. The best is a combination of the real place and a proper map.

I propose to you that we are in a place that is real, and in this place, there are mountains, valleys, and areas of wilderness. In this place are some cliffs and crags that could potentially cause us much harm, but also roads to unique places. So, yes, we are in a real place, but we also have a proper map for this place, and as I stated, the best thing is a combination. The best scenario is that we can be warned of the cliffs and how to avoid them. We can be warned of an up-and-coming mountain that we will have to climb or notified of a valley ahead where we might rest. Because of this combination, and if we look at it right, we can be on an incredible adventure here and blessed with our map in hand.

We can do our best to enjoy all that is here for us because, as I said, the best is a combination of the map and a real place. Our Bible is our map, so go out and enjoy the landscape, be warned of the mountains and cliffs, but also take a rest in the valleys. Enjoy the journey, find the roads to unique places, and read the map because the best is a combination.

THOUGHT 2. THE COWBOYS

Imagine with me if you will, you and I are seated in very good seats at the Dallas Cowboys football stadium and we are poised to watch the Cowboys play the New York Giants.

As I support my home team "The Cowboys" and as I cheer and motivate my chosen team, I notice that you are spending the majority of your time watching me.

After the first quarter you begin to ask me why I hate the New York Giants and by half time you are telling all those around you who will listen that my hatred for the Giants is offensive to you.

You then explain to me that the Cowboys paraphernalia that I am wearing is extremely offensive to you and that it should not be allowed to be worn or at least not be visible out of respect for Giants fans. I then begin to do my best to explain to you that I do not in any way hate the Giants, I am just a Dallas Cowboys fan, so therefore I support and believe in my team.

After the game you begin to pursue creating laws that will make it illegal for me to wear my Cowboys paraphernalia in a visible fashion, and that would make it against the law for me to cheer for or even speak the name of the Cowboys.

This of course seems completely ludicrous as I write these words, but this is exactly what goes on each day in our world regarding Christianity.

My prayer for you is that you would be just as proud of your chosen eternal team as you are of your chosen football team, and that you would not only be found being a courteous and kind pro football fan but also a courteous and kind Christian. Other people, other fans and other players are all around us and our example will be their guide. Go Christ and how bout them Cowboys.

THE SAVIOR

I stood there lost and empty handed
I stood there basking in my shame
I stood there mad and empty headed
Wondering why I was in pain

I had heard of this forgiveness
He had done for others just not me
I was reminded at each Christmas
I had gone to far to be set free.

Through the years I heard His call
I couldn't imagine it included me
All I knew was of all my falls
How could He ever set me free?

The weight of all that had happened
The depth of tragedy and my sin
The memories just put a cap on
The thought He'd never let me in.

Shame had handed me the bricks
That I built into a perfect wall.
I had fallen for all the tricks
That kept me separate and small.

There was a moment of transition
As I sat there in my pain
He told me of just one condition
That would loose all of my chains

He said that He had sent a savior
And for all my sins He did die
If I would just accept this loving offer
I'd live eternally with Him on high.

I through my failures at His feet
And I asked him to be my Lord
He said my son you're now complete
You'll live with me forever more.

So, if you're standing empty handed
If you're basking in your shame
If you're thinking you are too far gone
Please let me redirect your aim.

The Savior died for the sins of all
Past, present, future, and yours
Don't be the only reason you fall
Just come and lay down all your chores

He's ready to be your Savior
He is ready to be your friend
Just accept the sacrifice and favor
He will surely let you in
He will surely let you in.

BIBLIOGRAPHY

New International Version. (2011). BibleGateway.
com. http://www.biblegateway.com/versions/

New King James Version. BibleGateway.com.
http://www.biblegateway.com/versions/

Printed in the United States
by Baker & Taylor Publisher Services